After the
DIGGING

After the DIGGING

ALAN SHAPIRO

With a new Afterword

The University of Chicago Press
Chicago and London

ALAN SHAPIRO is professor of English and creative writing at the University
of North Carolina at Chapel Hill. He is the author of five books of poetry,
including *Mixed Company,* which won the 1996 *Los Angeles Times* prize for
poetry. His prose works include *Vigil* (1997) and *The Last Happy Occasion,*
which was a finalist for the 1996 National Book Critics Circle award for
biography/autobiography.

Some of these poems have appeared in the following magazines:
Canto: Night Seasons; Passage Out
Gramercy Review: Hands of Compassionate Women; Phantom Game;
    Ploughing
Poetry: Randolf Routh to Charles Trevelyan; The Dublin Evening Mail;
    Captain Wynne to Randolf Routh

The University of Chicago Press, Chicago 60637
The University of Chicago Press, Ltd., London
© 1981, 1998 by Alan Shapiro
All rights reserved. Originally published 1981
University of Chicago Press Edition 1998
Printed in the United States of America
07 06 05 04 03 02 01 00 99 98   1 2 3 4 5

ISBN: 0-226-75041-8 (paper)

Library of Congress Cataloging-in-Publication Data

Shapiro, Alan, 1952–
    After the digging / Alan Shapiro. — University of Chicago Press ed.
    p. cm.
    ISBN 0-226-75041-8 (pbk. : alk. paper)
    1. Famines—Ireland—Poetry.   2. Puritans—New England—Poetry.
I. Title.
PS3569.H338A69   1998
811′.54—dc21   98-14056
                                                                        CIP

⊗ The paper used in this publication meets the minimum requirements of
the American National Standard for Information Sciences—Permanence
of Paper for Printed Library Materials, ANSI Z39.48-1992.

for Carol Ann

Contents

I.

AFTER THE DIGGING

(A Sequence of Poems on the Irish Famine 1846-1849)

RANDOLF ROUTH TO CHARLES TREVELYAN

—September 6, 1846

Dear Sir, the harvest, such as it will be,
will be here soon. Yet we know it is Summer
only by the calendar. The rain
falls in unebbing tides, making each day
a darkness that the light illuminates.
Sir, the reports which come in every day
are not, as you suggest, exaggerations:
from Giant's Causeway to Cape Clear, from Dublin
to Galway Bay, the cold fires of disaster
burn through the green fields and each black plant blooms
luxuriant as an abundant harvest.

The people do starve
                    peaceably, as yet.
But how much longer, how much longer?
                                    Armed
with spades, a horde of paupers entered Cork—
"So thin," the officer in charge has written,
"I could not tell which ones were men, and which
were spades, except the spades looked sturdier."
They demanded food, and work. And when dispersed,
"Would that the government would send us food
instead of troops," one of them muttered, while
the rest like phantoms in an eerie silence
went off.
          Last week, outside of Erris where
the poor like crows swarm, combing the black fields,
living on nettles, weeds, and cabbage leaves,
women and children plundered a meal cart,
fifteen of them tearing at the sacks;
enlivened rags, numb to the drivers' whips,

3

too weak to drag the sacks off, or to scream,
they hobbled away, clutching to themselves
only small handfuls of the precious stuff.

Please do not think me impudent. Like you
I feel no great affection for the Irish.
But it is not enough that "we should tell them
they suffer from the providence of God";
or that "in terms of economic law
it's beneficial that the price of grain
should rise in proportion to the drop in wage."
We can no longer answer cries of want
with quoting economics, or with prayer.
Ireland is not, and never can be, Whitehall.
And while they starve, no Englishman is safe.

Sir, you have said yourself, "The evil here
with which we must contend is not the famine,
but their turbulent and selfish character,"
which I half think Nature herself condemns:
today, as if from the Old Testament—
with thunder beating on the iron clouds
which do not bend—the electricity
strikes with the bright and jagged edge of judgment,
while over each blighted field a dense fog falls
cold and damp and close, without any wind.

MEMORANDUM: On the Selling and Preparing of Indian Corn
          To the Officers of the Relief Commission
          From Charles Trevelyan
                    —*November 12, 1846*

Supplies have now been purchased to relieve
those whose distress derives exclusively
from the potato blight, and not to those
whose suffering is but ordinary want.
This distinction must be clearly kept.

     When our own food grew scarce as gold
         They sold at no cheap rate
     Indian Corn to the penniless.
         So gold was what we ate—

     A flint-hard gold that would carve fire
         As it entered our insides;
     The lucky ones would vomit it;
         The ones who didn't, died.

The proper method is to grind it twice.
Yet we should not give more than wholesome food.
Depending on our charity is not
to be made an agreeable mode of life.
Unground, it can afford a decent diet.

     We ate it while long lines of ships
         Of barley, oats, and wheat
     Floated in convoy down the Shannon
         Guarded by our Queen's fleet.

     When children ate, an alchemy
         Which left want unassuaged
     Transformed them right before our eyes
         To the angles of old age—

It can be soaked all night, uncrushed, in warm water,
then boiled for at least an hour and a half,
and eaten with some salt, or milk, if at hand.
Ten pounds of meal prepared this way
should feed a laboring man for seven days.

> Their yellowed, rickety, small hands;
>   Hair growing on their chins;
> While they fed on each golden blade
>   Each gold blade fed on them.

> Then from our bones, the parched skin swelled
>   Past human form, with heat,
> And we became pure forms of pain—
>   Who could only starve, not eat.

THE DUBLIN EVENING MAIL

—December 6, 1846

CLARE
This afternoon a gruesome incident,
not unfamiliar in these parts, occurred:
Captain Wynne's Inspector of the Works,
a Mr. Pearson Hennessey, incurred
near fatal wounds as he approached Clare Abbey.
He was accompanied by his chief clerk
and five foot soldiers—three in front of him
and two behind—when a man dressed in a skirt,
with blackened face, walked slowly from a ditch
and fired his blunderbuss at Hennessey,
who fell back in great torture.
                              The man bowed,
or rather as the clerk reports, curtsied
telling the others, "I mean *ye* no harm."

Shocked by his monstrous crime, and almost gay,
disarmingly good manners, no one tried
to apprehend him as he walked away.
Yet, fearing to be shot themselves, they ran
while Mr. Hennessey, without assistance,
with eighty shots lodged in his body, crawled
into the village.
                 And the peasants danced
as if it were a circus that approached,
aplauding the poor man like fiends in hell,
and, when he pleaded for a doctor, joked
"Sure, now ye are a beggar like ourselves."

CAPTAIN WYNNE TO RANDOLF ROUTH

—December 24, 1846

Dear Randolf, since the shooting incident
my staff is greatly agitated, and
I fear won't hold together for much longer.
They all seem waiting for the right excuse
to go—Tom Webb has gone and his successor,
Mr. MacBride (whom those who still can curse
call Mr. Hennessey), has left already.
Mr. Pratt's resigned, and Mr. Gamble
(the engineer in charge) thinks Millet's life
is threatened, and is going to remove him.

We must resume the works. Though this suspension
be the only armor we possess
against the bullet of assassins, still
something must be done. I have myself
inspected the small hamlets in the parish
and would describe to you what I have witnessed,
but anything you picture to yourself
which still enables you to kiss your wife,
embrace your son, and sleep until you wake,
is not what I have seen, nor what I felt.
But I must tell you something nonetheless.

Since even nettles now have all been eaten,
or buried in the snow—the snow which now
alone must feed the peasants, and keep them warm—
each hamlet is entirely deserted.
I counted fifteen corpses on the road,
like crops the living were too weak to plant:
the only earth upon them was the snow,
a few sticks, and small stones.

8

                                And no sounds came
from any of the hovels that I passed.
And it occurs to me, in retrospect,
that those poor wretches must have heard me coming
and knowing that (as I must now confess)
I looked upon starvation as disease,
kept quiet as a trap to draw me in,
hoping to sicken me. And I was sickened:

In one small hut I saw six human beings
crouched in a corner in some filthy straw:
four had once been children, but now wore
the anxious look of premature old age;
the other two, their parents I presume,
for though as thin as children, they were taller.
As I approached I realized the father
was the only one alive, for he was moaning
low and demonically, and his legs twitched—
though not enough to move, or move the others
who leant upon him still as if in death
they still cried for the help he could not give.

I hurried off, and faces stared at me
from every window that I passed, faces
whose eyes hunger had magnified, whose lips—
the last soft flesh upon them—were as blue
as the new snow and were speaking God knows what,
soundless as in a dream . . . what were they speaking?
Tell me, Randolf, what words they uttered, words
which every night are riddling my dreams,
which I wake up to; tell me what they mean.

And tell me when the works will be resumed.
Consider, Randolf, what I have recited;
I am a match for almost anything

I meet with here, but this I cannot stand.
Consider it, for something must be done.
And trust I speak sincerely when I say
I hope the winter finds you well, and please
pass on warmest regards to Randolf Junior,
and kiss your dear wife once for me.

Yours, Wynne.

THE LAST GUEST

—Saturday, August 3, 1849

(On Friday, the Queen touched Irish soil for the first time in
history, at the small harbor town of Cove. In honor of the occasion, the
town was renamed Queenstown. But this morning, Saturday, while the
Queen and her entourage proceed up to Cork and then to Waterford,
only one reporter for the London *Times* remains and is himself now
being driven to a steamship that will carry him up to Dublin to cover the
Queen's reception there. He remarks to his driver that the town's
lugubrious appearance affords an extraordinary contrast to the
excitement that crowded upon the streets the night before. And his
driver responds.)

Sir, you are right in your remark: today
Cove does not look the way it looked last night.
But then last night our dear Queen's royal yacht
and her fleet made a forest of our harbor.
Now only one ship bobs on these fierce waves,
one ship about to take you up to Dublin.
But never have we seen such sights: blue flares
across the sky; and on the scarlet cloths
draping each roof, the shamrock, rose, and thistle;
and bonfires masking the surrounding hills,
bringing a flood of light upon the town—
Cove is, indeed, unlike the place it was.
Why, this hill we are passing by, that's now
as black as if some huge piece of the night
remained as a memento of our joy:
this hill is E. B. Roche's, an MP from Cork.
Up there a bonfire 14 acres wide
(14 acres of his fir plantation)
rose like a new sun, brighter than any bomb,
which must have pleased Her Majesty—
though not as much as it had pleased his servants
who, with some tar and kindling, set it off

11

to show the Queen the great depths of their love,
and, no doubt, show the same to Mr. Roche.

Cove hardly is the place it was last night.
But truth be known last night I couldn't tell
if this was Cove. Now it is but itself.
These sprigs of laurel, and these flowery wreaths
festooning our small houses now are ours:
last night they made it seem our only trouble
was how to be gay, or that we thought our Queen
putting her lovely feet upon this shore
would make lush garlands spring out of the soil.
But look, on our doors now what spoils and withers
are decorations our fields always wear,
bits of the harvest we must eat all winter.
And these triumphal arches we pass under—
stripped of their sere and leaves by these slow men
down to what, if you weren't here last night,
would look more like the scaffolds just erected
for the victims of a revolution—they're now
all of triumph we have ever known.

Last night, in Queenstown, we may have been the hosts.
But here today, in Cove, we are the servants
we have always been, whose lives are but
a getting ready for great guests, and then
a cleaning up after the guests have gone.
And you, Sir, are the last to leave.
                                        The sea
looks mean enough, alright. But sure, your passage
to Dublin will be safe. And if the sea

does roughen till you are discomforted,
think of the festivities that await you there,
that our Queen brings with her, wherever she goes;
think of them for comfort, for they will be
surely as grand for you, as they were here.

PASSAGE OUT

(The log of Thomas Preston, captain of the brig *Temperance*
carrying Irish emigrants to Canada in the year of 1847)

JUNE 1

This good wind which has not let up
makes reaching Canada in six
or seven weeks conceivable.
And for our tattered Irish cargo
I pray we do. Our food will not
last any longer. As it is,
each person gets but seven pounds
of meal a week, which I have had
to ration daily. For I fear
these passengers, already being
in such a wretched state, would surely
consume at once all their provisions.

Almost none of them seem fit
for any travel. Most were sick
when we embarked, and some were starving.
Yet all were medically examined,
if one can call it that. They filed
one by one in quick succession
before a window, from which a doctor
glanced at their tongues, and took their money.
So frightened were they, filing past
with their tongues out and eyes shut tight,
it almost seemed they were receiving
communion and not passage out.
And yet so destitute perhaps

the only grace they now expect
is passage out.
                    The brig itself
seemed like the new world they were seeking
as they climbed slowly up the planks,
up to the deck and, from the railing,
waved triumphant to their loved ones
whose cries rose up as much from fear
as grief, because they stayed behind
to turn back, exiled, to their homes.

JUNE 7

Every day, from four to seven,
they come out of the hold and bicker,
crowding around the wooden stove
like gulls around a midden heap.
The ones with salted meat or herring,
the wealthy ones, keep frantic guard,
scalding their hands on the bright coals,
pushing the other hands away;
while the weak ones curse them to the grave
and shove till they are beaten back,
till they can grab their own turn, and
push back those weaker than themselves.
The young, the old, the most infirm,
mere rivals for each other's food:
even a pregnant woman—cursed
for the space her belly occupied—
was struck so hard that my first mate,
he had to bring her to my wife
who tends her now, free of her kin.
For there's no kin from four to seven,
no 'Irish' fighting at the stove—
just creatures who are suffering.
And then at seven from the shrouds
Jack pours some water on the fire,
and from the steam's hot surf they take
their half-cooked food down to the hold.

JUNE 12

Kittens. Today I think of kittens,
my cousin Dorothy's when she
was but a child. Her cat had littered
four kittens among which there was one
identical to all the rest
except the grain across its tongue
turned out, not in. So everything
it tried to eat with all its might
sucking at its mother's teat,
sucking for its life,
                              that grain forbid.
And for the two days till it died
the sweet milk stained its muzzle white.
Dorothy asked, "How could God do
such things?" And I cannot recall
how I replied. But I can guess,
today, what I would say to her.

Our water's running low: two casks
have started leaking and a third
which (now we know) held wine has turned
the water into vinegar.
Thus, I've had to reduce our rations.
And those with salted food—their last
remaining wealth—though they must starve,
have had to throw it overboard
for eating it brings on a thirst
their water cannot satisfy.

In the distant sky, all afternoon,
we saw great combs of rain appear
and vanish, and appear, too far

17

for hope, yet too close not to see.
Then later the wind stopped.

                            And now
the ocean stiller than a pond,
marooned, I hear her ask that question
and I know what I would say to her.

JUNE 20

Ship fever, faster than a fire,
has broken out. And over fifty
of the hundred shut up in the dark,
unventilated hold are dying.
The "Mistress," as my wife is called,
tends whom she can but can do little.
More than to ease their agony,
she quiets it, with laudanum.
Still, "Mistress, please, for God's sake, water"
rises with the effluvium,
the shroud of stench that can be seen,
but not breathed, covering the deck.

JUNE 23

A deputation came on deck,
fifteen or more, demanding water
for their sick ones below. Said they
would rush the store and help themselves;
"Are we to drink the diarrhoea?"
As helpless as they were enraged,
most could not even make a fist
or raise their arms.
                    One cruel mate seeing
but a relief from tedium
laughed at their threats and, for form's sake,
fired his gun into the air.
And the great bang hit them like a shot.
Some fell down to their knees, and begged;
the rest turned, climbing through the hatch
meekly, to face their families.

19

JUNE 27

The dead are going overboard
without prayer, and with little sorrow
(for few have life enough for grief).
Like spoiled meat, husbands, wives, and children
thrown overboard into the deep—
as if this were their last kind act
that now they can relieve their kin
who have at last when they lie down
some room to change position in.

JULY 9

At noon a brig about two miles
off starboard bow came into view.
And I am sure we looked to them
as they to us: serene against
the glister of the soft, green waves,
sunlight glinting off the bow,
the sails like blossoms on the wind
full as the white clouds, and as new.

JULY 30
Gross Isle, Canada

The foul mattresses, huge barrels
of vilest matter, the rags and clothes
dumped from the ships that came before us,
dumped in this river that is now
undrinkable, this water we
for weeks have dreamed of.
                        When we anchored
the doctor came on board and said,
"Ha, there is fever here," and left.
And since then, now almost a week,
only the dead are brought to shore.
The rest must wait till there is room
for quarantine.
                        So from the brig
we watch while large and graceful ships
from Germany glide past with ease
bearing the robust passengers
on to their precious days. Cruel
the way they sing, the girls who laugh—
their blond hair shining in the sun—
laughing as they blow kisses to
these blighted shades who stagger out
of the dark hold, pained by the light.

AUGUST 10

After the digging, Sean McGuire,
his skin too papery to sweat,
drove two shovels into the ground
making a cross, and said, "By this,
Mary, I swear I will go back
as soon as I earn passage home
and murder him that murdered you,
our landlord, Palmerston."
                                        And went,
like all the rest, like living refuse
half naked, maimed, to Montreal,
to Boston, to New York; the seeds
of typhus already blossoming.

And blossoming those other seeds
as virulent as a disease,
that grief which suffering can't feel,
that will return as surely as
the seasons when the flesh returns.
Who have endured must now endure
a healing no less unbearable,
must be consoled by hate's cold feel
fixing all their memories
into a purpose stronger than life,
immutable as loss.
                              They go,
and may God go with them who bring
into the new world nothing else
but epitaphs for legacies.

II.

CAPTIVITIES

(Poems on the New England Puritans)

—They want to get out of themselves and escape from the man. That is madness: instead of changing into angels, they change into beasts. . . .
—Montaigne

HANDS OF COMPASSIONATE WOMEN: Lam. 4,10

—A woman of Boston Congregation, having been in much trouble of
mind about her spiritual estate, at length grew into utter desperation,
and could not endure to hear of any comfort, etc., so as one day she took
her infant and threw it into a well, and then came into the house and
said, now she was sure she should be damned for she had drowned her
child. . . .   —*from John Winthrop's journal*
                                                              August, 1637

Good friends and neighbors, I have come to tell you
(for I can see this now, now that I see)
that my intolerable twilight's over,
dissolved just as the Lord intended always.
Though palsied with the love I bore my child,
its small elusive good, I somehow felt
hope rising like the erratic exaltation
of larks in that vast pause before a storm.
But now all hope is stiller than a flame
no breathing frets. And I am almost calm
and, in a way, upright.
                          Oh how I hoped
then as I watched my child thrive day by day,
her flesh soft as a light upon her bones,
the warm light of the Lord. And so at first
I, loving her, praised Him. I prayed that since
she was so godly, surely I was God's,
surely He made my love His dwelling place.
And then the thought, as quiet as the quick
stealth of a thief, took shape in me, that He
could not love Jesus more than I loved her.
Then all my praising stopped.
                          My child sickened,
faded with judgment, grew well like a sign,

25

shifted from His dark Word to His light
and back again. I drew back from her cries
as from a devils' chorus, hymning of sins
so deep they never could be named, or known.
I prayed myself to sleep each night and dreamt
another child, peevish because neglected,
tugged at my sleeve until I noticed him
who when I turned to notice turned away.
Throughout that awful twilight my little babe
was but the scripture of God's mood toward me,
the righteous reflex of a righteous love—
was hard and crooked where I was perverse,
shifting in and out of Hell, until today.
For I awoke, sensing a certain sweetness,
a kind of grace, and knew my trial was ending.

I have been cast out of God's furnace now,
as He once cast the child out of my loins,
much as I cast the child, my only hope,
my only child, this morning, into a well.
But I have come to tell you, you good people,
that when I heard her small weight hit, her one
brief cry, I felt—as you may never feel—
that what He hath intended hath been done,
and praised Him for the light He took away,
and praised Him because I knew, at last, that I
was damned, and that the dark was comforting.

26

NIGHT SEASONS: The Captivity of Mary Rowlandson

(Taken by the Wamponoags under King Philip in February, 1676,
and restored three months later.)

> I will make my arrows drunk with blood,
>   and my sword shall devour flesh—
> with the blood of the slain and the captives,
>   from the long-haired heads of the enemy.
> —*Deuteronomy 32.42*

When Indians descended on your town,
emerging from the tree bark and the leaves
in a thick hail of bullets, hatchets, spears
glittering and swift, howling with awful joy—
it was the wilderness itself, ungodly,
sent of God, that came for you. It was
your Egypt, Goodwife Rowlandson, your time.
To His hard mercy God had called you out.
And seeing your house burn, children scattered, feeling
blood running down the daughter clinging to you,
you felt your faith turn at His call into
a hammer that could not let up, that worked
over and over at everything He sent you.
Nothing occurred that you did not deserve
or was not just: at even your poor babe's
"I shall die, I shall die" you struck and struck
till, lying with her corpse all through that night,
not letting go until they stripped her, stiff
and blue, out of your arms, you thought how once
you could not bear the sight of death, and now
even its smell was sweet, and savory.

You waited on the Lord by waiting on
your captors, sewing in exchange for food:

27

horse hoof or ear, a fawn so young its bones
were meat. In even the flintiest bread, in mould,
tree bark, or skunk you looked for God, to taste
His grace. And His Word, which you fed upon,
would bring, in one hand, honey from the rock
of what you ate and leave you, in the other,
fed and unsatisfied, blood on your mouth.
Through the wild waters of the world, forsaken,
and gathered, and forsaken again, by Him
whose thoughts were not your thoughts, nor His ways yours,
you would forget inside the master's wigwam
and, dreaming upon the past, would suddenly
run out to your loved ones, the Christian world
in which you thought you had walked righteously,
finding only those devils, thick as trees,
yourself among them, searching for the sins
for which the Lord's Hand touched you, in His way.

He brought you home when you were ready. Then
and ever after, working in your thoughts
through each night season of the night, you felt
Him whose eye waketh ever, watching you.
You learned the vanity of things too well.
So with your family fast asleep about you
you must have thought of them, through your wild tears,
what careless thoughts their smallest dreams released;
heard each insect ticking in the wood
with much too dry a sound; and must have known
'afflicted' was the meaning of salvation,
knowing that you had been, and were, and would be
loved because chastened, scourged because received.

PHANTOM GAME

—Salem Village, January 1692

His heavy musket slung across one shoulder,
the rum flask, empty now, across the other,
Ezekial Upton sees the evening bring
·a darkening current out of trees and thickets
and, in the Lord's distemper, His thorough chill,
give evil sight to what he cannot see.

All day he tramped through blue snow in the forest,
through clearings where, more like another sun,
bright as the cloths of Christ, the snow would burst
like punishment into his eyes.
       All day
he hunted phantom game, saw when he fired
deer like a dark flash flit between the birches,
vanish into the wild, unholy quiet
that deepened more the more it was disturbed.

Twined in the wickered light and shadow, all day
a kind of diligent elusiveness
moved through the thickets when he moved,
         and watched him.

And it is watching now as he tramps home—
everything around him that he cannot see
and sees, that he cannot hear and hears.
         He fires
into the sudden shudder of a bush
and up from where he thought a heathen crouched

wings rise and scatter.
                    He will think of this
come spring, when through the village
                    What place, whose heart
outside the Sainthood is not wilderness?

the same elusive game against the Lamb
will rage.
              He will remember all of it
when those poor girls, their necks wrenched like an owl's,
across the full moon of their tortured sight
will see the evil flash, will see it vanish
into the thickets of his neighbor's eyes.
Oh when their words rise like a flood of light
naming the names
              The Lamb and His followers
the dragon and his
              Ezekial Upton
will recall it all: the dropsy that had killed
three cows; his land each year becoming more
and more tight-fisted than a merchant's hand;
the daydreams of the kindness of cruel women.
Soon he will hear them say
                    Susanna Martin,
Bridget Bishop, Sarah Good . . .
                    And after,
thinking with something much like second sight,

The Lamb and His followers, the dragon and his

will, all too clearly, make it all make sense.

30

PLOUGHING

—The Father of Lies uttered an awful Truth when he said through the mouth of a possessed man, *If God would give me leave I would find enough in the best of you all to make you all mine.*

—*Cotton Mather*

Through Salem, as if spring were merely spring
and not the Prince of Power's atmosphere,
the catkins swell, shedding in every breeze
a small bright storm; white blossoms break like grace;
and here and there on Goodman Upton's farm
through whose hard heart all day he ploughs, wild flowers
like little suns appear.
                              Wherever he works
mosquitoes and black flies—small devils wild
with the scent of blood, that river that is sin—
hymn distantly as hell into his ears
and now and then he slaps at where he feels,
brushing his skin, their almost spectral legs.
Moment by moment he learns vigilance.
Moment by moment through the trees and bushes
birds weave their shadow of dark purposes,
which he ignores, keeping to his plough;
keeps ploughing till, suddenly coming toward him,
one of them breaks, jewel-like, into the light:

Is it the same bird that the girls can see
high on a beam inside the Meeting House
sucking between the fingers of the Saint,
his good friend Martha Cory?
                              Though he could not
see where the Black Man whispered at her ear,

nor see her specter where they pointed, screaming,
"Don't you hear the drum beat, Gospel Witch?
Why don't you go? Why don't you go? "
                                  he saw
how they lay struck dumb on the floor before her,
their bodies twisting like the rod of Moses,
their white tongues stretched to an ungodly length;
and when her hand, put to their cold flesh, drew
off her spectral hand, and they cried out,
"Cory, Cory, Cory,"
                  he saw the evil;
just as he sees above his own head now
that same bird dip and, like a fluttering light,
like clever reasoning,
                      circle away
from each stone that he hurls.
                      Who have the girls
cried out upon today?
                  His plough strikes rock,
jolting away the reins and, his hands burning,
and stumbling to his knees as if he heard
deep in the hedges the spade-foot frogs begin
to sound too much like drumming in his ears,
he tries with all his might to say the Lord's Prayer
but, having learned that everywhere is Egypt,
listens as he recalls,
                Let him that thinketh
he standeth safe take heed now, lest he fall.

A LITTLE DUST

—To see such a one gashed and gored though it were done by other
hands will effect our hearts if they be not harder than the stones, and
more flinty than the rocks. But much more when our consciences tell us
that our cruel hands have made these wounds, and the bloody
instruments by which our friends were gored were of our own forging.
                           —*Samuel Parris, minister of Salem Village*
                                                    September, 1693

The storm brought branches of the Resting Tree,
the great oak in the middle of the field,
down to the ground last night. And working toward it,
swinging your scythe which, like an answered prayer,
cut through this year's good harvest, the shining wheat,
the half moon glittering as it rose and fell—
you did not mind the branches tangled there,
the static fire of leaves, to be cleared away.
What could they be but His reminder that,
despite His blessing, your prosperity,
you were still Adam's son, tangled with sin?
So clearing them away meant clearing blame,
brushing from the white stone of your name
a little dust.
                    Yet you would find, today,
another meaning in that scheme of branches,
would see one branch hiss coldly as it slid
through slant light, through a ghostly fire of dust
would see its sharp head rise and, lithe with power,
the tongue strike in a nest of mice, their eyes
unopened, no hair upon their bodies;
in a moment, all of them were gone,

and all at once the air that had been blurred

as by a heat, a water glimmering,
vanished into the common air:
                              You saw
for the first time, how Satan's grip was nothing
but the belief that you would go untouched,
believing that your name was that White Stone
because you went unnamed.
                              You could walk home
and, by your bible, kneel down and confess;
and on the Sabbath hear your shame pronounced
while you stand, bowed as if upon the scaffold
where they, who had been neighbors only, stood.
But, Son of Adam, God would put no bright
coal to your lips, nor clothe in shining garments
the filthy ones that no one can cast off.
Although perhaps forgiven, your punishment
would be
              never to know it, always to yearn
as for a thing that is not to be found
again on earth,
                    the kisses of His mouth
for which the Lord says one must burn, for good.

Afterword

During the summer of 1978, I worked in the microfilm room of the old Stanford library. When no one was around, which was most of the time, I'd spend the better part of each workday reading through microfilm of nineteenth-century editions of the London *Times,* particularly the column called "The Irish Question," begun around 1846 in response to the Irish potato famine. What fascinated me was not so much the journalistic accounts of what was going on in Ireland, the suffering that the Irish endured between 1846 and 1849, but how the English perceived and responded to a devastation their own economic, social, and political policies had helped create and prolong. Around this time, as well, I had read *The Great Hunger* by Cecil Woodham-Smith; while the two together, the newspaper accounts and Woodham-Smith's graphic depiction and analysis of that catastrophe, comprised much of the materials, voices, and idioms I would use in composing the Irish section of *After the Digging,* the inspiration for all the poems in the book, the Puritan poems as well as the Irish ones, came from an essay by David Levin in his book, *In Defense of Historical Literature.*

The essay, "Historical Fact in Fiction and Drama," is an eloquent critique of Arthur Miller's play *The Crucible.* Levin takes Miller to task for a number of factual inaccuracies and aesthetic judgments that not only badly distort and simplify the historical event itself, but also reduce his characters in the play to moral ciphers. The heroes are so good, and the villains so evil, that the play ultimately reinforces the very black-or-white thinking it purportedly attacks. Levin is especially hard on Miller for his treatment of the witch-hunters, a treatment that develops "historically documented selfish motives and logical errors to grotesque extremes." "The witch-hunters in *The Crucible,*" according to Levin, "are so foolish, their logic so extremely burlesqued, their motives so badly temporal, that one may easily underestimate

35

the terrible implications of their mistakes. Stupid or vicious men's errors can be appalling; but the lesson would be even more appalling if one realized that intelligent men, who tried to be fair and saw the dangers in some of their methods, reached the same conclusions and enforced the same penalties."

My ambition in these poems was to explore how decent people can be brought to do indecent things. By adopting the personae of certain nineteenth-century English officials who observed the horrible consequences of their policies and attitudes, and various seventeenth-century New England Puritans blinded by fanatical obsession, I tried to dramatize and embody the fragility and contingency of moral norms, and the insidious ways perception, action, and intimate feeling are constrained, if not entirely determined, by the pressures of history. Of course, what made me want to write about these subjects and explore these questions were the many evils of our own century—the mass destruction of the First and Second World Wars, the Holocaust, the atomic bombs American warplanes dropped on Nagasaki and Hiroshima. Some of these subjects I have written about more directly in my subsequent work, in poems like "Mud Dancing" and "Virgil's Descent" from *Covenant,* and in "The Basement" from *Mixed Company.* In the context of these later poems, I hope the voices of the more recent dead will now be audible in the historically remote but still compelling voices brought together in this book.

Finally, I should also say that I would never have written either suite of poems had I not gone to Stanford and had the great good luck of studying with Donald Davie and Kenneth Fields. Despite the many differences between them as teachers and poets, both Davie and Fields shared a powerful distrust of the exclusive thinking which dominated the poetry of the sixties and seventies, a thinking which held that only free verse and its improvised rhythms could render faithfully the contours of contemporary life, that discursiveness and narrative were the domain of prose, not poetry, that the business of the poet was not to traffic in ideas or statements but to present and juxtapose images and feelings with as much intensity as possible. Twenty years ago, it seemed as if all subjects but personal experience had been given over to the novel or the essay, and all forms but free verse had been dismissed as obsolete. To Davie and Fields, however, the value of form, whether free or traditional, open or closed, depended entirely on what the form enabled you to say, and it was therefore, in their view, just as possible to write with passion and surprise in tight measures as it was to write mechanically in loose ones. More importantly, Davie and Fields encouraged their students to go against the grain of their inclinations and habits — to write in meter and rhyme if all they'd ever written was free verse; to read Oppen or Dorn, Pound, Bunting, or Ronald Johnson, if all they'd ever read were Winters and Cunningham. In a true spirit of experimentation, they encouraged their students to try to integrate, not choose between, what literary fashion told them should be kept apart.

Only in such an atmosphere of intellectual and aesthetic openness could I have had the confidence to pursue what in those days was such an unconventional project. Because Davie and Fields were scholars as well as poets, I didn't feel any sort of opposition between historical research and imaginative writing, between fidelity to facts and literary transformation. When I began work on the Puritan poems I therefore didn't hesitate to ask Jay Fliegelman, a professor of American literature, either for advice in how to hunt down primary source materials, or for criticism on the accuracy of the poems I eventually wrote. In fact, it was through Jay that I obtained microfilm of the sermons that Samuel Parrish delivered in Salem Village during the witchcraft hysteria, sermons which provided the poems with many of their details and much of their tone and language. Whatever virtue these poems may possess is due, in large part, to the example my Stanford teachers set for me, both in the classroom and on the page.

Alan Shapiro
February 1998